Country COTTAGES

Country
COTTAGES

CINDY SMITH COOPER

Hoffman Media
1900 International Park Drive, Suite 50
Birmingham, Alabama 35243
hoffmanmedia.com

83 PRESS

ISBN #978-1-940772-73-8
Printed in China

TABLE OF CONTENTS

INTRODUCTION

Country style is one of the most personal decorating genres that makes a universal connection. This style can be enjoyed in the middle of the city or in rural settings, accompanied with a desire for a simpler lifestyle and a pleasurable way of living—and a fondness for the patina of worn paint and handmade accessories. With our search to feature country cottages throughout the land, we found various architectural designs that preserve country style. From modern to shabby chic, the outdoor setting is oftentimes just as significant as the inside, from row gardens to rolling green backdrops.

For homeowners who love to entertain, country style lends a feeling of openness to guests. It blends informal with formal in fabrics, furniture, and lighting, as well as architectural design, and combines flea market finds with period antiques. Individual tastes in style found their origins in Europe and, as time went on, the American West.

Homes in the country cottage style can be found at water's edge or in the mountains, city, or suburbia. The country look has become essential to creating a home that meets modern standards and suits the needs of families as a refuge. By mixing antiques and collectibles—as well as flea market finds, heirloom linens and quilts, and even the occasional shed antlers—you can achieve the look plus enjoy the comfortable feel of country at its best. And, at its best, it is warm, forgiving, and filled with personal style!

Inside this book, you will find a portfolio of country cottages that live large and open new concepts for cozy living. Each home features details shared by interior designers, architects, or the homeowner themselves. From Washington to Michigan, the collection within these pages will introduce you to new ideas and fresh inspiration. Each room in every home tour is a personal story of a family living experience, whether built to welcome loved ones and guests or simply to prepare a cozy nest for two. From the kitchen to the back porch, country is a way of life—and home is always the ultimate retreat.

A House of Happy Chance

THE WELCOMING COMFORT OF RUSTIC CHARM AND THE RELAXED ELEGANCE OF SOPHISTICATED STYLE MAKE THE PERFECT PAIR IN THIS GETAWAY BY THE LAKE.

A country lake cottage tucked away on the banks of Skaneateles Lake in New York wasn't part of the plan for designer Thom Filicia, but a chance encounter with a "for sale" sign changed that. After stopping on a whim, the owner of Thom Filicia, Inc. saw the neglected colonial-style home for what it was: the perfect place to create a sanctuary just a few hours from the city. And because it was located near his childhood home in Syracuse, New York, the temptation was too great to resist.

He made the purchase and dove into the renovation, focusing on structural repairs and optimizing the flow of the layout. He took the opportunity to install additional doors and diamond-shaped windows, maximizing the views of the lake, offering better access to the water, and putting his own spin on the structure's rustic design.

Once the layout was complete, Thom turned his attention to designing an interior that would welcome friends and family and allow them to relax while enjoying the serenity of the lake. Careful to preserve rustic elements of the original design, like wooden paneling and five-plank doors, he introduced notes of Shingle, Greek Revival, and colonial styles, tying them together with a modern thread that resulted in a comfortably sophisticated atmosphere.

Since every room is used for entertaining, coffee tables and ottomans in the living spaces accommodate drinks, plates, and guests, and each design choice works together to put visitors at complete ease. In the living room, where a stone fireplace offers warmth on cooler nights, the woven wall coverings, rough-hewn ceiling beams, and layered rugs cocoon the space in rich, comforting texture, encouraging guests to cozy up on the furniture that balances the more traditional elements with a taste of modern style.

It's a similar experience in the sunroom, where Thom retained the original bark log but balanced it with black walls trimmed in crisp white. A sleek-lined, tufted bench paired with wide club chairs and a high-backed sofa inject a cozy spirit into the space, which was designed to encourage quiet conversation.

In fact, Thom created every part of the home for a purpose, down to delineating distinct areas of the kitchen. From preparing meals to sorting the mail, every task has a space, and every space flows together to form a design that expertly blends country with contemporary—all with a dash of nautical charm thrown in.

Functional additions—like heightened cabinets for extra storage and a bar where a side door used to be—helped make the most of every inch of the space, which means preparing for guests is a breeze. Country touches, like cabinet doors backed with chicken wire, bulkhead lights, ring pulls, and boat cleat cabinet pulls, add a subtle hint of the nautical influence that can be seen throughout the entire house.

Contributing to the focus Thom wanted to place on the outdoors, the dining room offers an eye-catching view of the lake beyond while showcasing Thom's expert use of color. Cobalt-blue linen lines the walls, creating a subtly textured background and tying in the Greek Peak chairs from the

Thom Filicia Home Collection. Overhead, the vaulted ceiling—discovered while Thom was installing speakers—is essential to the airy nature of the space, and the bright white shade only adds to the effect. Carrying it down to the trim, Thom enhanced the rich hue of the walls, and matching blue edging on the drapes achieved the tailored look he wanted for the space.

And no getaway by the lake would be complete without the inclusion of a bedroom designed for true relaxation, a task that Thom approached with the intention of crafting a peaceful and airy space. The home's underlying nautical spirit makes its appearance in the long, low planked ceiling and horizontal wall panels, which reminded Thom of the interior of an antique ship, but the room's design is grounded in layered textiles and rich, earthy tones. From the cracked earth patterned rug to the fabric-covered headboard and all the shades of blue in between, the space marries subtle sophistication with lush comfort for a thoroughly restful experience.

Outside, all of the coziness found within spills onto the lawn and beyond. From the deck to the dock, everywhere you look offers a place to enjoy the lake with loved ones. When the sun sets, guests gather around the fire pit and enjoy the view—not only of the water, but of the home that joined the family by chance.

As part of his attempt to create distinct spaces within the kitchen, Thom chose dark surfaces to delineate the "chef's domain." The color choice also adds a splash of moody atmosphere while serving the functional purpose of making spills less noticeable.

Some of the home's spaces take on a more vibrant personality, like the downstairs guest bedroom. Grounded by a four-poster bed in a rich finish, the room is livened up with bold stripes, whimsical throw pillows, and an eye-catching patterned wallpaper.

In the upstairs guest bedroom, Thom wanted to create a tailored, masculine atmosphere, which he did through the use of greens and gray-blues. Textured wallpaper in a sophisticated gray enhances the white ceiling and trim, which help the painted five-plank door pop.

As Thom wanted the home to encourage indoor/outdoor living, he put the same care and attention into the exterior living spaces that he put into the interior design. With a dock that makes for unforgettable entertaining on summer days and a fire pit that becomes a popular gathering spot once the sun goes down, the space reflects the designer's desire to connect the home to its surroundings.

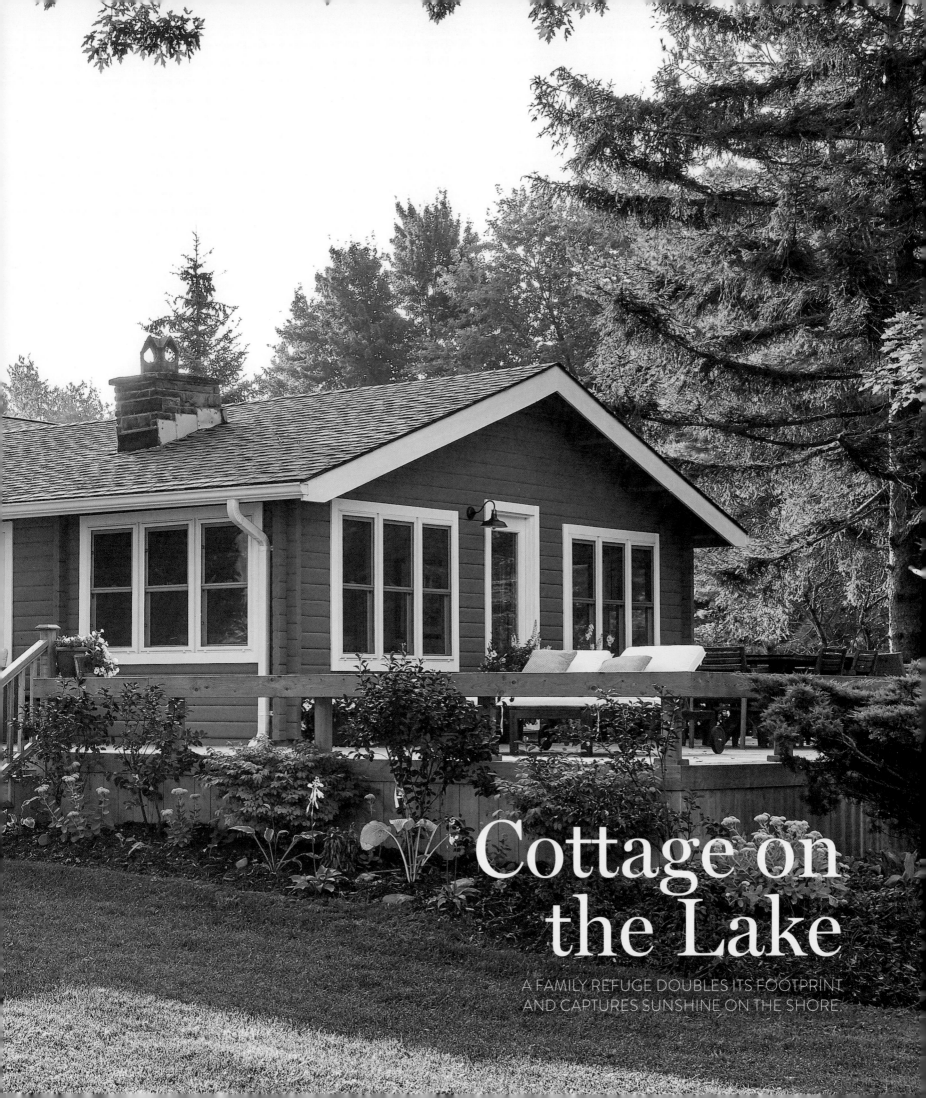

Cottage on the Lake

A FAMILY REFUGE DOUBLES ITS FOOTPRINT
AND CAPTURES SUNSHINE ON THE SHORE.

The original cottage, with its cedar logs and dark look, was transformed to a white, airy space, which helps the eye focus on the views. Original to the home, the solid cedar floors are softened by simple, natural fabrics like cotton drapery and linen bedding, which also add warmth.

The kitchen is designed for family and friends to crowd together in harmony and be able to enjoy views of the lake. A wall of cabinets was added with glass-fronted uppers to display the collection of blue pottery and serving dishes. Children can help set the table without entering the working part of the kitchen. The kitchen cabinets were designed by Croma and were custom-made by a local woodworker and friend of the family. The countertops are Carrara marble, drawers feature matte black hardware, and the sink has polished nickel plumbing fixtures. "We wanted to make sure that the materials used would age well from being well-loved during family gatherings," says Amy. "It was essential to us that the style look timeless and classic."

The new dining room is located where the original sunroom once stood. The narrow dining table pulls out to seat 12 to 14 people comfortably.

The wood-burning stone fireplace in the living room is original to the home and became a focal point once the surrounding walls and ceilings were painted white. The updated feature carries the warm tones from the shore and beach that sit below the cottage.

The cottage is perched on a bank above the lake, so views of the water and sunsets are panoramic and visible from almost every room. The landscaping is simple and classic, using white hydrangeas, lavender, lilacs, and white daisies, which provide natural materials for home-picked bouquets throughout the summer. The driveway winds through natural woods and meadows, which provide plenty of room for gardening during the year.

A Pan Abode log cottage that was built in 1969 sits on a hilltop on the shores of Lake Huron, Michigan, where a staircase connects the cottage to the beach. The family doubled the home's size with an addition that included a master suite, an additional bath for the children, and a laundry room. A serving pantry and center hall join the old and new sections. The original cottage was approximately 900 square feet, and the addition is the same. Amy Kent and Ryan Martin of Croma Design in Southwestern Ontario are the proud designers of a cherished place for Amy's family.

After the loss of Amy's father, she and her family—along with her brother, Bill, his family, and their mother, Shirley—found themselves visiting so often that everyone needed more room in the smaller getaway. Features from the original home Amy was accustomed to, like the master suite, center entry hall, serving pantry, and open kitchen for entertaining, were reconfigured as smaller spaces.

The comfortable living room includes a beam reclaimed from a nearby barn and installed as a mantel. The log walls have a defining vintage appearance contrasting with timeless cedar floors.

The custom-built cabinets and island provide plenty of workspace, and the windows over the counter offer views of the lake.

Seating for twelve is easily attained in this dining room that also allows plenty of natural light. A vintage glass cabinet showcases family keepsakes and curiosities.

In the master bedroom, the flooring was engineered with an oiled finish that matches the existing wood floor. Wall paneling was added to create a seamless transition from the old to the new and carry over the character from the log half of the cottage. While the master does not face the lake, the light colors and water-related accents lend a consistent feel, even without the lake views.

The bunk room was designed to accommodate two sets of granddaughters so they could grow up sharing this cottage experience each summer. It is the largest bedroom in the original part of the cottage, so there is room for them to play and even invite friends for sleepovers. The palette is feminine but light and simple, so it will grow with them over time.

The guest room is quite small but has the best views of the water. Furnishings were kept simple with an antique bed in a dark green, breezy linen fabrics, and wall sconces.

HURON
ONTARIO
MICHIGAN
ERIE
SUPERIOR

The deck wraps around three sides of the cottage and doubles the living space. The deck wall holds plenty of hooks for hanging towels to dry after beach visits and also provides privacy for the outdoor shower on the other side.

A Serene Sanctuary

READY TO START A NEW PHASE OF THEIR LIFE, ONE COUPLE
FOUND A BREATH OF FRESH AIR IN GAINESVILLE, GEORGIA.

Newly an empty nester and recovering from a bout with cancer, Heidi Ferguson turned to building a new home in Georgia as a chance for a fresh start. "She had basically planned the whole house while she was in treatment," says designer Maggie Griffin. "She said it was like her saving grace while she was undergoing chemotherapy."

Hoping to create a calming sanctuary in which to start the next chapter of her life with her husband, Heidi enlisted Maggie's help in selecting elements such as the finishes and lighting fixtures. Together, they settled on a color palette dominated by white surfaces, which they accented with touches of black and soft blue tones.

After establishing a soothing, clean backdrop, Maggie focused on introducing an element of warmth that would balance that aspect of the design. "In any new-build situation, everything can kind of look so new that it's almost cold," she says. "So we brought in textures and soft finishes that would balance her beautiful, sleek floors, white shiplap walls, and tongue-and-groove ceilings."

They selected a plush powder blue sectional for the living area, setting the tone for the relaxing atmosphere the women wanted to create in the space. Comfy chairs, a tufted ottoman, and a thick-woven jute rug further soften the space, as does the natural glow from two sets of French doors set into one wall. "And then, over time, we have added more and more layers to her modern farmhouse look," Maggie adds.

Leaning more toward the modern end of that design style, the kitchen is, as Maggie puts it, "the jewel of the whole house." Gold pendant lights over the island, heavy barstools, and a custom Vent-A-Hood over the range contribute to an industrial style that is as functional as it is beautiful—which was important, considering Heidi's love of cooking.

"She loved the thought of keeping the kitchen so clean, and to me, it's very classic," Maggie says. To soften the white Shaker-style cabinets and marble-topped island, they pulled in an antique runner between the range and island. "It gives it such a warm touch and kind of reminds you that not everything is so brand new in the house."

Throughout the design process, Maggie encouraged Heidi to identify what she loved about the farmhouse style seen in the warm woods and layered textures and make it her own.

"So, where she had spent a significant amount of time planning this house with the help of Pinterest and Instagram and all the images we all see on a daily basis, she really trusted my professional opinion on how to make her house different than what she was seeing in all those images," she says.

The personalization is seen in the master bedroom, where a beaded chandelier hangs from a vaulted ceiling over a bed sided with flax fibers. Powder blue walls soften the shiplap for the soothing effect Heidi wanted to see. In the bedding, Maggie encouraged Heidi to go classic, leaving open the possibility of changing things up with throw pillows and blankets. "And if she tires of them, then she will still have a pretty white base to work with," she notes.

As in the rest of the home, color defers to layered textures like the jute rug on the floor and driftwood piece over the bed, injecting warmth into what could have been a cold space. "I think that my favorite part of the home is how warm and inviting the spaces are—that they feel immediately comfortable and charming, and it's a place where you really want to spend time," Maggie says.

From the finishes and lighting fixtures to the furniture and linens, every element of the home was layered with care to make everyone who enters want to linger. "I think that this house in particular feels very warm," Maggie adds. "And that has a lot to do with the people who live here, too."

Set against the shiplap wall, the bed in the master suite is upholstered in a flax linen that both softens the design and contributes a note of texture. "That kind of nubby linen is a very common thread throughout the house," Maggie says. "We used it in several areas, and to me, it kind of creates some cohesion against all of the white walls and the harder surfaces." She points out the lack of overpowering color or pattern in the room, stating, "I do think that the master bedroom is one of my favorite spaces because of how soothing the room is."

In the main powder room, Heidi agreed to let Maggie introduce a patterned wallpaper instead of sticking with the white walls seen throughout the rest of the home. "The wallpaper was a bolder move," Maggie says. "I encouraged her to balance that with the wainscoting, because it gave it a bit more of a cottage feel, and it wouldn't feel so overpowered with pattern."

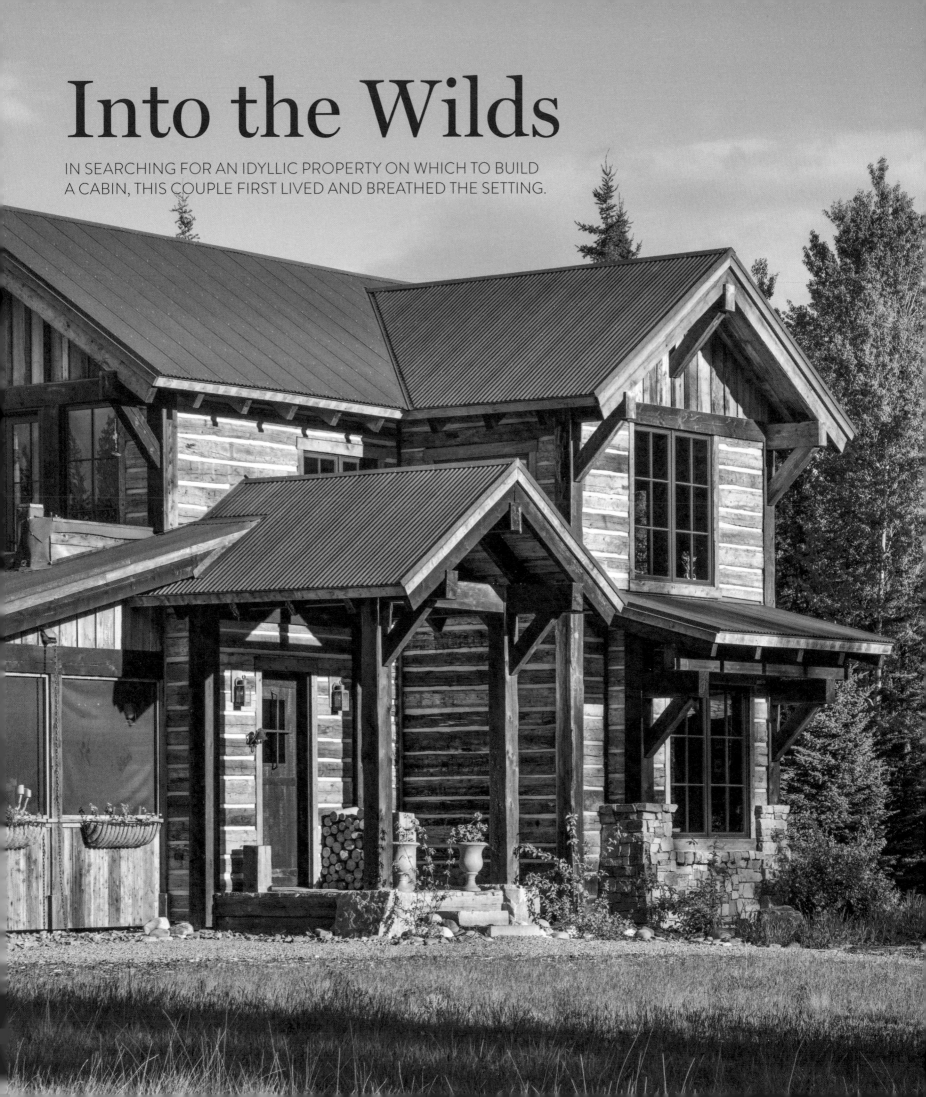

Into the Wilds

IN SEARCHING FOR AN IDYLLIC PROPERTY ON WHICH TO BUILD
A CABIN, THIS COUPLE FIRST LIVED AND BREATHED THE SETTING.

After spending time searching for the perfect location to build a rural Montana home, Chris Graff visited an 80-acre parcel at the suggestion of a Realtor. The requirements for the new build included proximity to a river and an off-the-grid location in order to allow Chris to live in the wilderness. Coincidentally, around the same time he saw the location, Chris met his wife, Monica, in Chicago—and the rest is history. While establishing their dream location, the couple lived in a yurt and began making their design plans for a reclaimed rustic home. It was their desire to have a place that "really appreciated the spirit of the homesteaders and their ideas," says Chris. Drywall would not be used; instead, they chose a mix of stone, reclaimed barnwood, beadboard, and salvaged logs from an old cabin as the materials of choice for constructing the home.

To site the location, careful attention was paid to the aesthetics, such as views of the mountains and construction of a cutthroat trout pond, and the essentials, like rigorous testing for septic permits, the ability to attract wildlife, and topography planning for potential floods.

Cozy and inviting on the inside, the home allows the Graffs to enjoy views of the wilderness and, at times, the sound of wolves in the moonlight or a moose wading through the little pond. At other times, spotted fawns are in view, but there is always a feeling of nature being absolutely magical in the surround.

Nooks and niches for reading provide a casual feel throughout the home. Rich fabrics in earth tones add the desired texture and warmth, while walls throughout are raw boards with only certain spaces bearing an off-white wash on beadboard for an aged look. Most furnishings are new but have a weathered quality.

Seating in the great room is for viewing the outdoors, and cream side chairs, a lush green velvet sofa, and rugs are layered for comfort. Shelving on either side of the large paned window frames the landscape much like a painting.

Off the great room, the kitchen has a homesteader feel, so various surfaces, finishes, doors, and hardware have an added-as-affordable appeal. Countertops are a mixture of a caramel-and-beige marble pattern and dark wood. The island area is made of wood stained a late-season huckleberry tone topped with a contrasting wood countertop. Woven rattan stools are convenient for views out of the windows surrounding the kitchen.

The dining area welcomes guests off the patio with seating for six and contrasting chair coverings that give the collected appeal of vintage style. In the galley off the side entrance, black-and-white images are framed from the couple's travels. Walls and ceilings are reclaimed wood and cream-washed beadboard. The Tom and Jerry–inspired mouse hole is for the family cats. Iron stair railings were crafted by a local artisan, giving the entrance and galley a distinctive character.

A variety of wood types used from the island to the pantry give the appliances a uniform look. A corrugated metal door slides to hide the organized pantry space for linens and food storage.

The master bath has a handmade cabinet with an enamel knob and side storage for towels. The shallow copper sink features a hammered finish and sits atop the honed-edge black onyx countertop. The mirror contrasts with the otherwise wood surroundings. Flooring is stained Douglas fir, reclaimed from the area. The copper tub sits atop a bed of river rock from Bali. Rustic copper finish pendants add an accent to the restful setting.

Framed images of surrounding scenic views hang over wrought-iron beds. Scrollwork patterned bedding beautifully complements the rustic chink-and-log walls.

Guests who spend the night can also stay in Monica's writing room with built-in daybed and bookshelves overlooking the pond. Rainbows viewed from this window can often be seen during the summer storms. Another bath connects with this second guest room with a similar custom-made shelf for storage and cream beadboard accents. The adjacent powder room features a sink basin made from a salvaged coal bucket from a New York City subway.

Screened and open porches with furnishings like the small table and benches or rocking chairs allow time outdoors for quiet reflection and wildlife viewing.

Neutral, Naturally

A MODERN COUNTRY ABODE INVITES
GUESTS TO RETREAT IN RELAXED STYLE.

Among the rolling hills of the Tennessee countryside, this family found the perfect setting for their home. Consulting with designer Kara Blalock of ReFresh Home, they requested an interior of neutrals with splashes of white and gold. The extensive use of neutrals gave Kara the freedom to layer textures and many natural elements. Incorporating stone, wood, and marble touches was key to the look, as were stain-resistant fabrics in slipcovered furniture for comfort and charm.

The living room's soft palette and focus on TV viewing meant that all of the furnishings needed to be casual and family friendly. The tone-on-tone linen and mohair accent pillows give a cozy comfortable feel, while uniform ceramic fireballs add contemporary charm in the fireplace. The entire home uses custom-made white linen curtains with a subtle texture. Antique books and collectible pieces flank either side of the fireplace along with other wood, glass, and metal accessories for interest.

The kitchen, living, and dining rooms are all open to allow the family to entertain a crowd and share time together. In the dining area, the mirrored console table brings a touch of elegance, while chunky candlesticks and other accessories give a clean, no-fuss feel to the area.

In the sitting room, white twill covers the slipcovered sofa. Mixed media artwork from a local artist and the light fixture were both treasured pieces. The homeowner brought them into their new home as design inspiration, including them as cherished keepsakes. Kara carried out the interior style in the room by including plaids, stripes, and florals with accent accessories.

The Belgian linen sofa and seating in the family room is complemented by a neutral buffalo check print and striped pillows. The side table and gold lantern-style chandelier add a touch of gold. This niche was a perfect spot to add an indoor swing, used as a reading nook. This unique area provides a relaxed spot for a quiet respite with a cowhide throw rug underneath.

Chosen for its comfort and ease in maintenance, the slipcovered furniture provides the perfect solution for an active family. Accents of tone-on-tone and mohair pillows provide extra spots to nestle by the fireplace.

The sitting room features a tufted bench used as a coffee table and placed on a mohair rug. A cozy striped chair and slipcovered side chairs are accessorized with throw pillows featuring neutral floral patterns and beads sewn on in a chevron pattern.

Cowhides are easy to care for and a fun addition to the country look. They can be swept, vacuumed, and even hosed down if needed. Collected and vintage hides are frequently heirlooms and are prized by their owners.

Just for fun, the indoor swing adds a quiet niche and touches of gold in the room add a bit of bling to contrast with the linen sofa with buffalo plaid and striped pillows.

Layered bedding with various textures adds interest and a luxurious feel for visitors in the guest room. Side tables were brought from a previous home and are a sentimental addition to the room. Opposite, left: A reclaimed barn door was used as the headboard in the son's room. Repurposed pieces are often great solutions for a rustic feel and, with the addition of neutral plaid and beige bedding, create a comfortable refuge for rest.

An open-air effect with a view of the countryside provides all-seasons appeal. Entertaining guests at any temperature is possible using retractable large screens to the outside.

Worth the Wait

A RENOVATION AIMED AT PRESERVING THE PAST
ONLY ADDED TO THIS HOME'S STORIED HISTORY.

Set against the side of the main structure, the diamond window in the post office shows off the original siding of the historical home.

Years before Sandra Schpoont and her husband, Steve Axelrod, purchased their property in Chilmark, Massachusetts, a teenaged Sandra admired the home from the seat of her bicycle, never dreaming it would eventually belong to her. But when she and her family rented the Martha's Vineyard cottage one summer five years ago, they fell in love. Two years later, they made an offer.

In addition to the main house, built in 1880, they found themselves the owners of a barn, a shed, and what was once the original post office for one of the local communities. "It's a really cool property, because it has a lot of history, and it's very beautiful, and it's in a really unique location," Sandra says, noting the viewing platform on the property that offers an iconic view of the island's southern shore.

But before they could settle in, they needed to turn the outdated structures into something truly habitable. "It hadn't been renovated in many, many years," Sandra says. A lack of heat and insulation was only one of the challenges they faced, which included an outdated kitchen, broken windows, and floors eaten away by pests. "We knew that we had to put a lot of work into the house to make it livable."

So, they started over. Hiring Sullivan and Associates Architects for the renovation, they gutted the first floor of the main structure and rearranged the entire layout to include the addition of a pantry, laundry area, office, and master suite.

Throughout the process, they worked within the guidelines of local zoning and historical boards, as well as their own desire to "maintain the integrity of the house," says Sandra. As a result, the various structures on the property seem to belong together, and that sense of cohesion continues into the interior, where Sandra wanted to create a "more modern-looking farmhouse," rather than a typical Cape Cod cottage.

For that, she turned to husband-and-wife team Keren and Thomas Richter of design studio White Arrow, who had never visited Martha's Vineyard prior to joining the project. But armed with a design aesthetic that immediately attracted Sandra, the couple jumped in.

In the same way the renovation married the property's history with new spaces and updated amenities, the Richters paired classic elements with global influences and layered textures for a unique atmosphere rich with carefully composed contrasts. In the living room, a white-planked ceiling hangs over a Tuareg rug from Morocco, atop which sits a coffee table and sapphire-hued sofa ordered from Australia.

The blue tone threads itself through the rest of the house, appearing in places like the Lacanche range in the kitchen—a must for Steve. It's these kinds of details that help keep the design from leaning nautical, while creative lighting choices inject pops of contemporary flair into more classic surroundings.

The contrast is strikingly evident in the room that once served as a post office, where extra care was taken to preserve the rustic charm original to the space. Sandra and Steve opted not to insulate the walls, settling for a fresh coat of white paint on the natural wood to freshen and lighten the room, and left the original windows along one wall untouched. The one-room structure found its contemporary facelift in pieces like the George Nakashima coffee table passed down from Sandra's parents.

And despite the fact that it's a new addition, the master suite carries the same charm as the rest of the home. Designed to offer the couple meadow and water views, it delivers on its promise—both inside and out. Lit from a bank of windows and an overhead dormer, the space is the perfect balance of white surfaces, natural tones, and interesting details.

Original artwork and a Moroccan rug offer color and warmth, and the bed, Sandra notes, is from Australia. And although—much like Sandra's happy ending with this home—it took a long time to come, she acknowledges that, in the end, "it was really worth it."

Working with architect Chuck Sullivan and builders Thomas Van Hollebeke and Jared Kent, the interior designers set about translating Sandra's ideas into the perfect space for getting away from the homeowners' Brooklyn residence. "We were very, very lucky, because we had a great architect, great builders, and great designers" Sandra says.

Since Sandra wanted one room in the home that was dark, the designers painted the office a deep blue hue. The shade is offset by white window casings and ceiling planks, as well as a lighter wash on the floor.

Introducing most of the color in the master bedroom, the painting on the wall was created by artist Karl Klingbiel, who is a friend of Sandra's.

Before the renovation, the original shed housed bunk beds for the previous owners' teenaged kids. "But we decided that it wasn't really useful for our purposes," Sandra says, "so we gutted it and turned it into a sweet little cottage." The bed that now resides in the structure boasts a headboard made from the original floors from the main house, and a window overhead fills the space with a natural glow.

Built to Last

LOCATED ON THE BEAUTIFUL COASTLINE OF THE
PUGET SOUND, THIS RUSTIC ABODE WAS CONSTRUCTED
TO BE A FAMILY HOME FOR YEARS TO COME.

A gorgeous mix of industrial and rustic styles with touches of sophistication interspersed throughout, this open-concept beach home is the result of years of the homeowners' vacations to Whidbey Island, Washington. A beloved area to the family, the sand-covered shores of Puget Sound are both beautiful and perilous at times, which makes the design of this home even more interesting.

Working sustainably, architect and owner of Hoedemaker Pfeiffer, LLC, Steve Hoedemaker created the house to be able to withstand the sometimes-harsh conditions of the area. To start, he raised the overall structure by just a few feet to allow water to move freely below in case of flooding. He placed the many windows and doors strategically around the house not only to allow ventilation on warmer days, but also to protect from sea spray on stormy days. A durable zinc roof acts as a safeguard against the rough weather as well.

Inside, Steve continued the practical yet pretty motif. Concrete floors were the perfect choice not only for their durability in high traffic but also because they complement the white-washed wood planks along the walls and ceilings. They used precast concrete for the two fireplaces that sit at either end of the great room.

The homeowners wanted a design that allowed for family and friends to move freely throughout the home, so Steve employed the concept of two cabins and one great room. A large living space with a dining area, two sitting spaces, and a kitchen are flanked by two wings with a loft and water views—one wing is for the homeowners, and the other is for guests.

Large wood beams line the tall ceiling of the great room, with high windows that let natural light stream in from above. Throughout the home, interior designer Paula Alvarez of PB Designs included hints of nautical motifs to allude to the homeowner's long-standing love of the area. In the great room, beacon-style lights hang from above in between the wood beams, and a large painting of crashing waves sits above the fireplace. A coffee table and end tables in one of the sitting areas feature weathered wood surfaces, reminiscent of rustic driftwood outside, and a large wooden oar crowns the center set of French doors.

As expected, another important feature of the home was the view. Steve's design allows for views of Puget Sound from every angle of the great room, thanks to the wall lined with windows and three sets of French doors. In the charming kitchen area, two small windows flank a French range. To keep sight lines open, Steve opted for open shelving in the upper cabinetry.

The home's casually elegant style beckons friends and family in, but it's the practicality of the space that keeps people coming back year-round. "Above all, this is a structure designed to be durable and private, but also warm and welcoming," Steve says. "Combining the look and feel of a well-worn boathouse with all of the luxuries of home, it is built to last and to age with grace."

To give the homeowners gorgeous views of the shoreline, Steve designed the great room to have double-height ceilings. It's the only space in the home that has them and allowed for the addition of the rustic wood beams.

The great room of the home was an architectual feat, as it's such a large space that fulfills many functions. Steve created two separate sitting spaces and a dining space in the middle across from the kitchen to give the easiest access and best flow for the family.

While much of the home is designed with practical choices, the homeowners did opt for a few luxury items, such as the Carrara marble countertops and many Oushak rugs throughout the residence.

Steve designed the home so that every bedroom has views of Puget Sound. Paula echoed the scenery with deep blue throw pillows and white linen bedding.

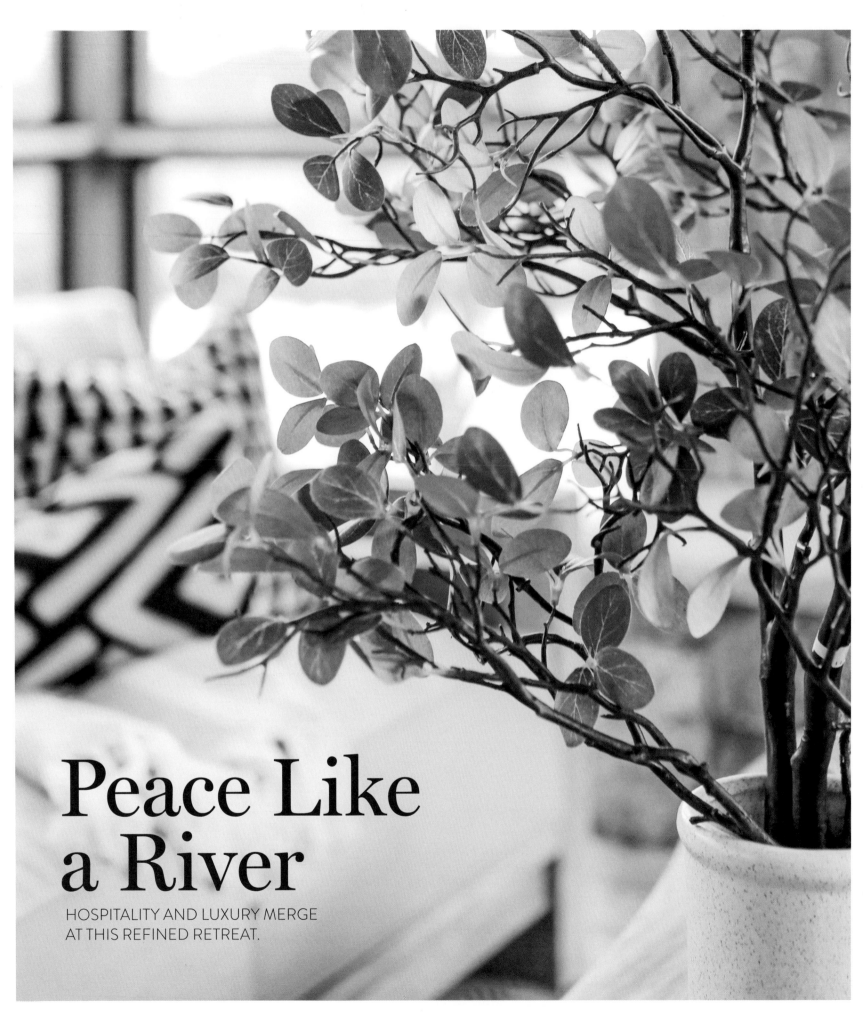

Peace Like a River

HOSPITALITY AND LUXURY MERGE
AT THIS REFINED RETREAT.

Abundant wildlife, open fields, and natural beauty mark the area between the Volunteer State's Duck and Tennessee Rivers. It's here, too, that this homeowner, a builder and avid outdoorsman, desired a restorative getaway, where his large extended family could retreat for weekends of dove hunting, fly fishing, and, perhaps most importantly, memory-making.

The challenge was to bring natural elements indoors while keeping the overall aesthetic of the cabin clean and refined. Principal Designer Connie Vernich of Vernich Interiors was selected for the job, and the result of her vision was this modern-rustic cabin that idyllically complements its lush location.

While the open floor plan can easily accommodate large groups, the integration of deep, comfortable seating areas throughout the home helps maximize the coziness of the cottage. Soaring windows let gleaming light pour in, while rustic beams, Tennessee limestone, and a rich array of browns and grays balance out the crisp, whitewashed walls. A hand-carved wood coffee table accents the living room, adding texture to the symmetric space, while oversize art pulls the palette altogether.

A magnificent driftwood console table anchors this striking vignette, while woven baskets carry the eye up as they climb the paneled wall.

Meanwhile, the kitchen is up to the task of effortless entertaining. Under tapered metal pendant lights, a cascading waterfall island serves as a modern focal point, while a trio of plush stools ensures there's plenty of room to settle in and tell tales of the day's adventures. Oak cabinets, stained to a deep mocha, display serving pieces, and a fully stocked wine bar stands ready for spontaneous hosting.

The adjacent open-concept dining room is an impressive marriage of mixed materials, featuring metals, wood, fabric, and rattan. After a meal, guests can mingle by the fire on the grand porch, where the view is sure to outshine whatever's on the screen.

When it's time to retire, three bedrooms, plus a bonus bunk room for six, accommodate the weariest of sportsmen. In the master suite, a modern-rustic bed and a woven headboard and bench give layers of texture to these cozy quarters. Nearby, plush animal mounts add whimsy above a child's bed, while a pair of sleek white horns grace another sleeping space. Each guest room includes clever storage areas, such as sleek under-bed drawers, to help visitors feel right at home.

Exuding peace and comfort, and a reflection of the natural beauty in which it sits, the cottage's welcoming accommodations and luxurious amenities ensure it will serve as a beloved gathering place for many years to come.

With a family of avid hunters, the homeowner knew he would be hosting for frequent gatherings—especially the anticipated opening day of dove season, a highly social occasion. The kitchen's neutral palette and layers of natural textures, plus its stocked bar and oversize island, make this an especially welcoming hub for entertaining.

Sweeping scenic views set a majestic background for this elegant master suite, where a dramatic canopy bed layered with rich linens becomes a focal point of the space. Although the room's palette matches the wooded oasis outdoors, the designer chose geometric lines for the drapery panels, bed, and rug, an interesting contrast to nature's more organic growth.

What a way to welcome the wee ones: Whimsical animals greet visitors in a guest room specifically designed with kids in mind. Next door, a more mature style makes grown-up travelers feel right at home. Throughout the cottage, many interior doors are painted a coordinating charcoal. This adds warmth by breaking up the whitewashed walls.

Make room for the masses! Decked in charcoal and white, three sets of identical bunks offer a clever way to tuck in guests without sacrificing space. (Right) Knowing that his cottage would be a haven for entertaining, the homeowner desired a variety of deep, comfortable seating areas situated throughout the house.

What's the best seat in the house? Perhaps this scenic spot, where a duo of deep sofas give guests a front-row view of Mother Nature.

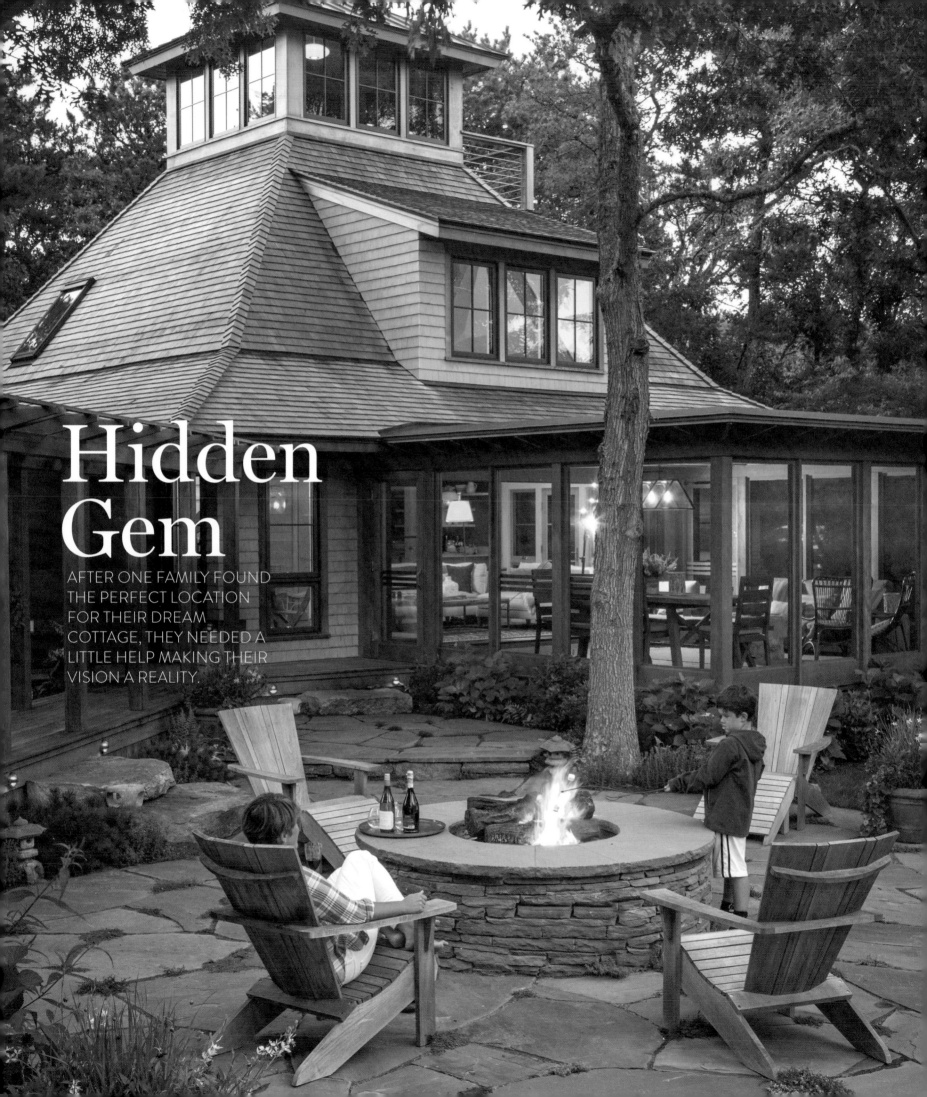

Hidden Gem

AFTER ONE FAMILY FOUND
THE PERFECT LOCATION
FOR THEIR DREAM
COTTAGE, THEY NEEDED A
LITTLE HELP MAKING THEIR
VISION A REALITY.

For a family with two growing boys, an isolated cottage nestled in the woods of Edgartown, Massachusetts, seemed like the perfect place to create a cozy getaway. But when it came to the cottage itself—as well as the guest cottage connected by a walkway—things weren't quite as picture perfect.

"The space was really limited," says architect Chuck Sullivan, who homeowner Becky Kidder brought in to update the dark, cramped space. When he arrived, he found small, closed-in spaces with an outdated style and a layout in severe need of reworking. He set about designing a layout that would create additional space for the family, as well as make better use of the space that existed.

"They wanted to be able to accommodate their family in the main structure and then have the secondary cottage act as a guest space," Chuck says. He addressed the special needs by adding an entryway, dormers, and a screened-in porch to the main structure, looking for creative ways to use every nook and cranny of the cottage.

Rather than the original closed-in stairway hidden at the back of the house, the new design features an open staircase lined with cable railing for an updated look. This detail continues up along the loft, opening the view down onto the living spaces from the second floor. Chuck tucked a bar beneath the stairs in his attempt to, as he says, "create usefulness in every part of the house."

But an open layout and functional design choices were only the beginning. Chuck chose a honey-toned fir lumber and antique heart pine for the interior beams and planking, whitewashing the wood to inject a soft warmth throughout the cottage. The finish offers a subtle contrast against the plaster and the casings, which Chuck says were painted a crisp white to give the design "a cleaner, simpler look." He notes that the doors and windows were left natural, creating the illusion of larger openings and connecting the space to the outdoors.

The material choices set the stage for a design that combines classic country-style elements, like wood paneling with contemporary details. Industrial-style chairs surround a breakfast table backed by a cozy banquette, which follows the trend of making the most of every corner. An oceanscape on the wall pulls in the rich blue tones that interior designer Mary Rentschler introduced throughout the home, popping against the classic neutral backdrop and adding an edge to an otherwise calm design.

The spirit of the home takes a more rustic turn in the screened-in porch, which connects to the main living area through a twelve-foot opening, extending the available space. Natural wood keeps the room warm, and the low ceiling contributes to the intimate, cozy atmosphere. "The idea was to make a room where you could be in the living room and interact with people on the screened porch and not feel a separation," Chuck says. A farmhouse table along one wall offers additional space for entertaining, and a nearby seating area welcomes guests over for after-dinner coffee.

In the master bedroom, Chuck installed built-ins instead of a closet to keep the space feeling open, and a patterned wallpaper adds depth to the clean, uncluttered design. The master bathroom features a deep blue penny tile and patterned wallpaper paired with planked ceilings, adding visual interest in a way that makes the small space feel large.

When the sun goes down, the family moves outside, where a fire pit awaits roasted marshmallows and quality time. Natural-edged bluestone lends an organic feel to the area, blurring the line between the yard and the surrounding woods and reminding the family why they fell in love with this hidden gem.

Wooden planking in the bar area adds warmth and texture to the space, balancing the sleek design of the cable railing Chuck chose. Overhead, a planked ceiling contrasts with the painted plaster of the home's walls.

From the master suite to the guest cottage, patterned wallpapers featuring bold, creative designs inject a lively spirit into the rooms and complement the classic, country-style elements throughout the home.

Throughout the design process, Chuck focused on creating practical, usable spaces that would enrich the family's experience in the home. Additions like the screened-in porch encourage fun among family and friends alike.

Gathering Place

INTENDED TO ESCAPE THE CHAOS OFF THE SHORE, THIS SEATTLE-AREA RETREAT FEATURES THE BEAUTY OF THE OUTDOORS AND RUSTIC INTERIORS THAT ECHO IT.

Tucked away off the coast of Washington sits a retreat like no other. Part vacation home, part adult summer camp, this Whidbey Island property is a welcoming haven from the busy inland life.

Once a quaint beach cabin, the original home on the property went through decades of disjointed renovations that left the house in a confused state. To address the puzzle of a property, the homeowners brought in Seattle-based design firm Hoedemaker Pfeiffer, LLC. "This project shows what happens when you focus on your strengths, defy convention, and take a few risks," co-owner of Hoedemaker Pfeiffer and architect Steve Hoedemaker explains. The team started by demolishing half of the original house, leaving only the original 1920s beach cabin and a great room added on during the 1970s, though the initial impression was to tear down the entire structure. They took an impressively modest approach to the demolition, opting to use whatever they could from the original cabin.

From there, the new design started to take hold. The original beach cabin turned into a dining hall that features a beach stone fireplace and large kitchen. The bathrooms are also included in the 1920s cottage structure. Steve opted for a camp-style bathroom with a few different showers, toilets, and sinks, and with an additional set of sinks outside the house.

For the great room, Steve and interior designer and co-owner of Hoedemaker Pfeiffer, LLC, Tim Pfeiffer added a loft for additional sleeping space and second fireplace. Inspired by both rustic park lodges and "surf chic," Tim brought in vintage-style surfboards and a lighting fixture made of glass balls covered in nautical netting. The furniture of the space leans more country, with a variety of rich leather armchairs and a tribal patterned rug to anchor the space.

The most unique part of the property, inimitable wall tents surround the cottage and act as bedrooms for the homeowners and their many guests. Outfitted with a variety of furnishings from all along the West Coast and abroad, the

Architect Steve Hoedemaker and designer Tim Pfeiffer expanded the deck of the original structure to allow family and friends to gather and enjoy the views.

tents have a unifying country theme but each with their own personality. In response to the cream canvas palette of the tent, Tim brought in rustic natural wood and rich, earthy hues for a true feel of the Pacific Northwest. Natural log beds are a recurring element throughout many of the rooms, along with vintage-style trunks, cowhide-covered pieces, and more tribal patterns.

Nestled in the woods behind the home, the field house is the cherry on top of the camp-style sundae. The structure is complete with a large pavilion gathering spot flanked by two cozy living rooms. Sticking with their local approach, Steve and Tim sourced all the Douglas fir and cedar from the Pacific Northwest, while the stone is from nearby Vancouver Island. One of the great rooms acts as a sunroom, with windows and benches along the walls. A large globe light fixture brings the eye upward. The other living room is the perfect spot for hot cocoa on a chilly night, with benches lining the walls and a small fireplace in the middle.

The intent of the homeowners was clear from the start and shows in the entire property's design: togetherness. Each space is cozy enough for a few to feel comfortable but large enough to host as many as the homeowners want—a feat, as any designer would attest. Even with all the space, it's not hard to imagine that everyone would still end up together.

Part of the original home, the dining room balances rustic wood-paneled walls with an abundance of floor-to-ceiling windows and doors to keep the space fresh and light. While the wood harkens back to the 1920s cabin, the natural light updates the space.

Each tent features its own electric heater, making the rooms perfect nearly year-round. In total, the area can sleep eight guests with an additional six in the great room.

In response to the homeowners' love of the natural Pacific Northwest landscape, Steve and Tim designed the scenic fieldhouse to be surrounded by undeveloped land, including a meadow, a fruit orchard, wetland ponds, and a maintained field for sporting. In fact, the family and designers drew inspiration from Seattle's waterfront parks and structures designed by Ellsworth Storey.

Life on Cedar Hill

THIS COTTAGE IS BUILT AROUND THE ORIGINAL HOME,
PROVIDING WOODEN FLOORS AND BEAMS WITH CHARACTER.

Cedar Hill is a small community outside Nashville, Tennessee. Amid the rural setting lies a cattle farm and homestead long held as the place to meet, share memories, and visit during the holidays. Now farmed by the Hamiltons, it is cherished as part of their family heritage with many years of history documented in albums of photographs.

The small tenant house moved to the location in the late 1960s, and the cottage arrived at its current look through a series of renovation projects. The cottage is literally built around the original home, providing wooden floors and beams that add original character. The last major renovation in 2017 occurred with the advice of kitchen and bath designer Sarah Avery, allowing the homeowners to modernize the additions and give the house a final, cohesive design.

The Hamiltons wanted a clean, modern style, using a shade of paint throughout that was, as homeowner Teresa Hamilton says, "slightly off-white." Interior designer Julie Couch of Julie Couch Interiors partnered with the couple to incorporate a crisp look with the addition of pristine off-white window treatments throughout most of the home, with limited use of color in each room.

The living room is the exception—it has touches of dark burnt orange velvet pillows and lively Oriental lamps that coordinate well with the deep gray sofa. The great room has pairs of custom chairs on either side of the fireplace. The ceiling is made from wood milled from the farm to add a legacy feel to the home. A pair of side benches for extra seating sits below the old bullet-making table. The artwork is a menagerie of prints and collected gallery finds.

The kitchen features white marble countertops and light gray cabinets on one side with a dark wood counter mount. Elongated iron drawer and cabinet pulls accessorize the cabinetry. A porcelain farmhouse sink with a Living Finish brass faucet and white cabinetry throughout most of the kitchen add to the pristine look Teresa desired in her kitchen renovation. The central light fixture is a unique stick-like design made of brass. White subway tiles and a Wolf double oven and cooktop are along the opposite wall for cooking in style. Reclaimed planks in mixed widths feature square-cut nails and a honey-colored stain for a warm effect.

White oak flooring that used to be a carport covers the dining room area with table seating for eight. Double doors open out to the hardscape, where the family enjoys outdoor dining in the fall and spring. The large ceiling beam is from an old barn on the property and was salvaged to add a reclaimed touch to the room.

The office maintains a simple look, with a blue rug and a funky gray chandelier that Teresa says keeps working at home fun. Flanked by comfortable chairs for reading, the room has walnut flooring and a trio of Remington lithographs for the wall décor.

Light gray and white cabinetry adds graceful style in contrast to the white oak flooring, and a brass chandelier contributes textural interest above the island. The characteristics left from the original house are sentimental to the owners and were purposely preserved during several renovations to the home.

Upon entering the home, guests find a reading spot situated nearby. Book collections throughout the home were mostly amassed by the husband, as he is an avid reader who has purchased several first-edition books as keepsakes.

The soft gray cabinets in the master bath add a subtle touch of color. The tall, narrow window was added to allow views of horses in the fields beyond.

The master bedroom has a soft curtain-lined wall behind the headboard for the perfect window cover, and it coordinates with the multi-paned wall of windows. The light fixture is composed of tiny beads, along with reclaimed walnut flooring. An antique sofa owned by the grandfather has been carefully restored and re-covered with a Suzani patterned fabric.

The Dutch door to the mudroom was selected so pets can be in a safe area during the day. With its rattan basket organization and coat hooks, all is conducive to the neat and tidy storage of the miscellaneous gear necessary for an active farm life.

Views are the main attraction outside the home with a pool, patio for dining, and two spots for sitting by a warm firepit in the evening. The picket fencing around the home is an attractive cottage-style addition that frames the home.

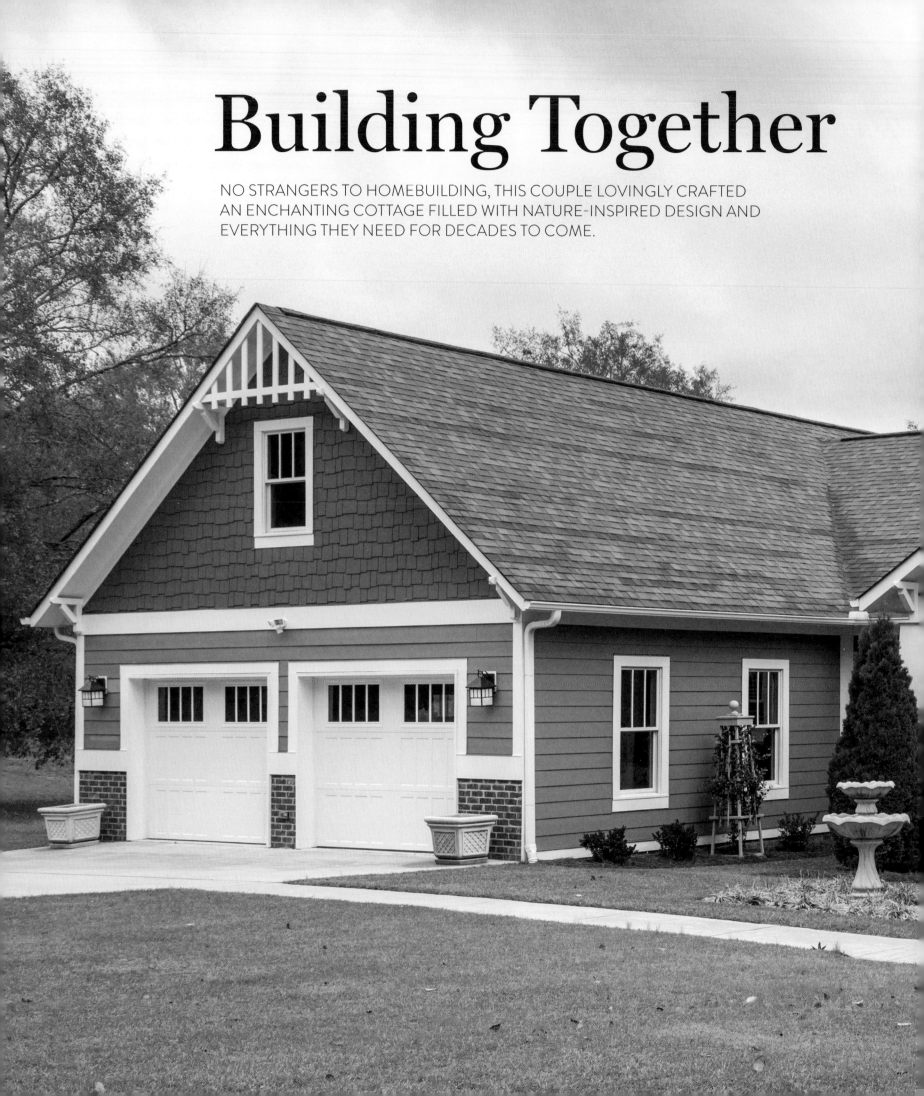

Building Together

NO STRANGERS TO HOMEBUILDING, THIS COUPLE LOVINGLY CRAFTED
AN ENCHANTING COTTAGE FILLED WITH NATURE-INSPIRED DESIGN AND
EVERYTHING THEY NEED FOR DECADES TO COME.

When you step into the entryway of the Flemings' charming craftsman cottage, you understand why it's Sonja Fleming's favorite part of the home. From the calming gray-green tone of the walls to the 11-foot-high coffered ceilings, every detail is a testament to the passion that she and her husband, Ronnie, have poured into every room.

Sonja notes that one of the foundations of their relationship is building together, adding that they have built two homes together in the past. Throughout the process of building their home, the couple have shared their progress on Instagram via @ourcraftsmancottage. "We're just one of those couples that loves homebuilding; we love projects, and we love working together doing this," Sonja says.

To create a home perfect for growing old in, the couple hired a contractor to create a layout featuring a single-level, open-concept cottage with wide doorways and high ceilings. Once the drywall was finished and the hardwood was installed, they got to work.

The result of their efforts is what Sonja calls a "fresh take on a craftsman," blending relaxing elements with all the charm of cottage style. The crisp white paneling and detailed trimwork in every room reveal Ronnie's skill as a finish carpenter, while the interior design was thoughtfully crafted by Sonja to echo the serene beauty of the outdoors. "I did a calmer green on the wall that would just have a fresh look to it," she says of the shade that she paired with Sandberg wallpaper throughout the house.

The outdoor influence was, in part, sparked by Sandra's collection of Spode Woodland dishes. "When I saw that pattern, I thought, 'I want this house to be about nature and

animals and the outdoors,'" she says. To that end, Sonja incorporated swaths of blue, brown, and green throughout the interior, complementing the shades with nature-inspired motifs and details, like landscape paintings.

Sonja found a balance for her love of color in the white-on-white design of the kitchen, where everything from the cabinets to the countertops to the backsplash features a crisp, clean finish. "I'm trying to create something that feels relaxing and peaceful and serene, so as much as I love color, I like to calm things back down a little bit by doing a lot of white everywhere," she says. She kept interest in the space with a subway tile backsplash and splashes of cheerful hues.

By the breakfast table, a selection of her Spode Woodland china collection is artfully displayed, highlighted by the brown tone of the buffalo check drapes. "I bought those dishes before I even knew what I was going to be doing with our cottage," Sonja says. "When I saw that pattern, I knew that was the feel that I wanted for our next home." Highlighting the home's underlying theme, the hydrangea pattern on the tablecloth ties the space together with the kitchen, where the same print is featured on the window treatment over the sink.

When it came to designing the master bedroom, Sonja wanted a space that wasn't overwhelmed with too much décor. "I just wanted it to be a place where, when I walk in, I feel totally relaxed," she says. To create drama without overpowering the space with accessories, Ronnie added paneling to the walls, and Sonja lifted an elegant headboard off the floor to elevate the eye toward the tray ceiling.

Outside, Sonja's love of nature has translated into a forest green exterior, while the white trim highlights the architectural details that make the home so special—like the tapered porch columns and ivy-covered latticework. And while Sonja and Ronnie have plenty of future plans for their home's exterior, for now, it's enough to enjoy the summer breezes from the front porch and remember all they have built together.

161

Cowtan & Tout's Rose and Hydrangea pattern decorates the table in the dining room, and lush greenery spills from a ceramic swan at the center of the table.

While white-on-white surfaces dominate the kitchen, the space is anything but boring. The Flemings' careful attention to detail is evident in everything from the herringbone pattern of the range backing to the walk-in pantry complete with beadboard and corbels, ensuring plenty of visual interest.

"I had to have my husband incorporate the paneled walls," Sonja says of the master bedroom. "I really cannot get enough of millwork; I'm hungry for craftsmanship and lots of texture in that way. So, just putting up paneled walls adds a lot of drama to a space without having to have a lot of accessories."

In the guest bedroom, Sonja added a creative focal point by hanging a collection of straw hats on the wall over the bed.

Home for the Family

THIS FAMILY-FOCUSED COUPLE CREATED A FRENCH-STYLE SANCTUARY FOR
THEIR KIDS, ACCENTED WITH MEMORIES FROM THEIR OWN CHILDHOODS.

171

When Elizabeth and Christopher Frost decided to renovate their kitchen a few years ago, they didn't have a specific style in mind. "We wanted something lighter than what we'd had," Elizabeth recalls. One thing was certain, though: it would be centered on their family.

The couple purchased the home in 2008, but it wasn't until years later that the idea to renovate popped into their heads. "It all started with some old cypress wood on [Elizabeth's] parents' farm," Christopher says about their kitchen redo. During a hurricane, Elizabeth's parents lost a few trees on their beloved family farm where she grew up. Instead of tossing the downed trees, though, her father decided to have them milled into wood planks. "Every time we visited, he told us we could have them, and when we decided to redo the kitchen, we centered all of it around that wood," Elizabeth says.

The Frosts' home was built in 1999, but the lot was originally planned and built on in the 1960s. The original house was later demolished and built over, but the large lot size stayed the same, something the couple loves.

To help with the renovation, the couple enlisted good friend and designer Shea Bryars. Knowing that bringing in the wood from the family farm was an important feature to the design, Shea decided to keep the rest of the kitchen fixtures light and airy. The cabinets were painted, and two different types of marble were installed, a more neutral finish on the perimeter countertops and Carrara marble on the island. The centerpiece, and Shea's favorite feature, comes into play over the stove. Hexagonal glass tiles with a dark grout create a statement as the backsplash, and a white range hood accented by a wood plank alludes to the reclaimed wood in the breakfast nook just a few feet over.

The breakfast nook is open to both the kitchen and the living room but is set off as its own space thanks to the milled wood from Elizabeth's family's farm. A large farmhouse table anchors the space, with a wall of windows accented with ticking stripe roman shades above the dining bench. An exquisite yet rustic chandelier hangs over the table.

As the couple started renovating the kitchen, the living room and dining room also fell into the mix. The family room now showcases French influence, even though the couple admits the style wasn't exactly what they were going for originally. "We knew we wanted a sophisticated cottage feel, but we didn't know exactly what style," Elizabeth says. "But now, I definitely see myself drawn to French style." Christopher adds, "I'd describe our style as French country. Not just French and not just country, but both together."

One of the most noticeable features of the home is the abundance of antiques. In every room, there's a piece with a story, from the pew in the kitchen that was a wedding gift to the bookcase from Christopher's parents to the art from Elizabeth's grandmother. "We're blessed to have heirlooms from both sides of the family," she says.

The emphasis on family is fitting for the Frosts. One of their most-loved features is the secluded street the home sits on, the perfect place for their children to play with friends. They designed every room with their three kids in mind. Even when Elizabeth describes her favorite part of the home, the kitchen, it comes back to her father and the farm. "I love having the kids coming in and out," she says, "and I can see the wood from my family, and it makes me think of them and so many memories I have with them."

Though the house fits into a French country style, Shea mixed in other elements throughout the home, like the industrial barstools in the kitchen and traditional Oriental rugs throughout the home.

The wooden pew sits prominently in the kitchen, in a small nook that was seemingly built for the piece that was a wedding gift.

In the dining room, a more ornate crystal-laden chandelier immediately catches the eye, followed by the antique china cabinet and vintage rug.

Elizabeth recalls that one of the reasons she fell in love with the home was the expansive backyard. The home also has a large porch that's perfect for family gatherings.

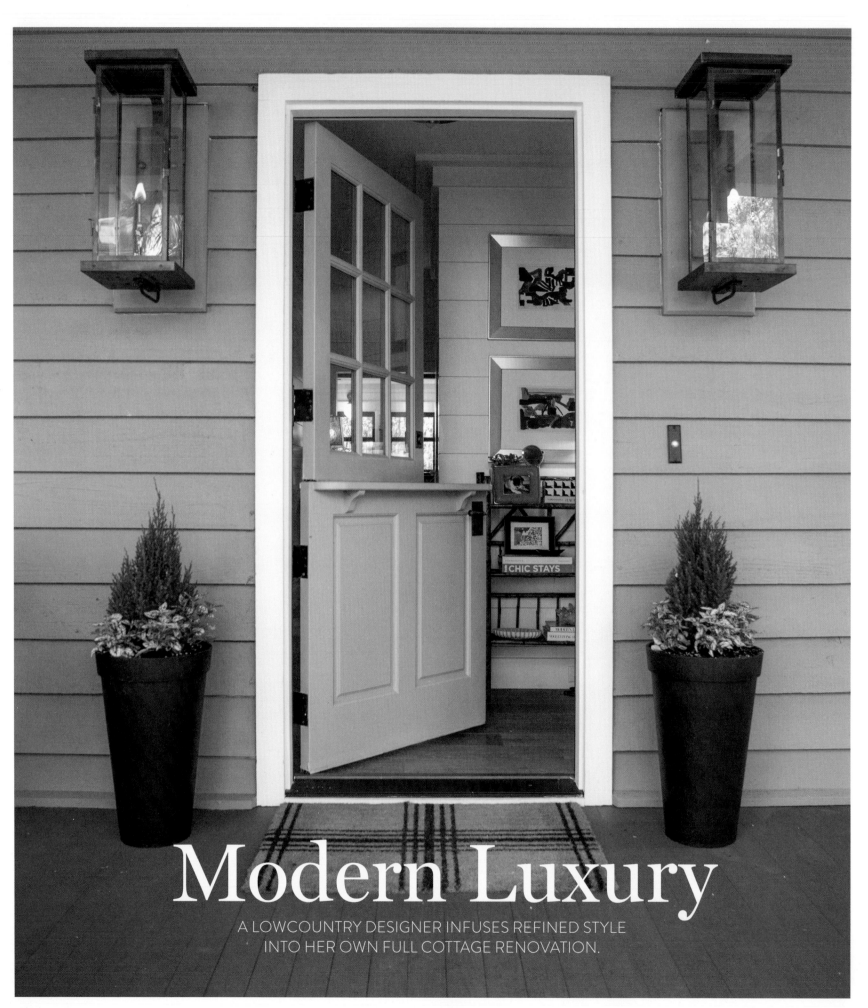

Modern Luxury

A LOWCOUNTRY DESIGNER INFUSES REFINED STYLE
INTO HER OWN FULL COTTAGE RENOVATION.

elley McRorie had the world at her fingertips when it came time to design her Lowcountry cottage. The award-winning principal of KS McRorie Interior Design had worked with luxury residential and hospitality clients for years, so she was particularly skilled at visioning tailored projects.

The sweet home she found sits on a tidal inlet of the May River in the historic district of Bluffton, South Carolina. "Because of the cottage's location and architecture, I wanted to remain true to the cottage aesthetic," Kelley says. "Rather than opening up the spaces by taking down walls, I actually added some walls and cased openings in the common areas."

Originally a three-bedroom, two-bathroom "true salt box," the house—which comes in at just under 2,000 square feet—was restructured to have one large master suite, while the other two bedrooms were converted to a den with full bath and a large walk-in closet. Additionally, Kelley took space out of the small attic to accommodate for a large master shower and chose to move the laundry room to the home's second floor.

Perhaps one of her most strikingly chic choices is the use of black cabinetry, a gorgeous departure from traditional coastal design. In the kitchen, Kelley cleverly added mirror fronts to help open up the especially small room. Meanwhile, custom brass and glass shelves atop the kitchen windows afford additional storage options for dishware.

While her curated furnishings are a sophisticated blend of new and antique, the designer's signature style seems to shine through her choices for walls and floors. Common areas of the home have wire-brushed white oak flooring, while Kelley selected wool carpeting for the den and gorgeous marble mosaics for both the mudroom and guest bath.

She also chose to expertly integrate unique wallcoverings throughout, from a deep-toned grass cloth in the den to Hermes in the master. Off the kitchen, the impeccable mudroom features the Italianate Nuvolette, an enduring Fornasetti design that "gives me joy every time I come home," Kelley says. For rooms without a wallcovering, she opted for a sleek butt board that amplifies the cottage charm.

"The house has eight-foot-high ceilings, so the combination of butt board, wood beam details, and wallcoverings helps to define the rooms but also slightly disguises the space issues," the homeowner explains. "Adding these elements actually helped make the house seem more spacious overall."

It was a long road to find the house, renovate, and settle in, but the result of Kelley's efforts is a perfect portfolio of her discriminating taste.

One of Kelley's favorite spaces is her living room, which features both her father's piano and a landscape diptych by Douglas Freeman, a well-known Southern artist and friend of the homeowner. Reclaimed wood beams are a focal feature of the room as well.

An elegant wet bar with a reclaimed wood top was fashioned into a small space that was previously an under-the-staircase closet. Formerly a galley kitchen, Kelley's charming dining nook maximizes its small space.

This heart of the home, a new addition during the renovation, packs plenty of style into its small footprint. The addition of mirrored fronts to the black cabinets opens up the space, while custom shelving adds storage without sacrificing sunlight. Crafted from reclaimed wood, the kitchen soffit mirrors the living room's beams.

By pulling space out of a small attic, the home's master suite was expanded to include a large shower. A luxurious jet-black tub with brass fixtures echoes the bespoke elements of the cottage's kitchen.

A New Story to Tell

A CENTURY-OLD CONNECTICUT COTTAGE
GETS A MODERN MAKEOVER

A modern floating shelf creates a clever drop zone without taking up precious space in the family's entryway. "The owner has a background in fashion and great style, so it was important for me to successfully reflect who she is," designer Melissa Lindsay says.

uilt in a storybook style beloved for its whimsical characteristics, this 1916 cottage attracted its owners with its pitched roof, its convenient location to New Canaan's downtown, and, no doubt, its undeniable charm. As an acclaimed interiors photographer, the wife also had impeccable style and a network of local professionals who could update the 100-year-old abode to reflect the family's more modern aesthetic.

Architect Louise Brooks, builder Rich Rosano, and designer Melissa Lindsay came up with a plan to open up the floor plan to maximize light and more easily accommodate children and pets. This included remodeling the kitchen, adding interesting architectural elements, and ultimately, giving the home a full facelift.

From there, the Pimlico Interiors designer had her hand in infusing classic sophistication. "The house had so much charm from the start," Melissa recalls, "we only had to amplify it." For her, this meant introducing modern elements throughout the home without overtaking its intrinsically traditional characteristics. For example, the team painted all of the walls bright white, which filled the home with warm natural light and made the old overscale windows pop. And since they couldn't re-stain the 100-year-old floors, Melissa suggested preserving them and painting them white as well.

In the kitchen, a local artist painted an oversize geometric pattern in a subtle beige and gray. The modern floor flows beautifully into the mudroom, which was painted a dark driftwood tone to set it apart. Open shelving in these areas highlights collections—both the practical and the pretty.

Throughout the home, the decor's neutral palette is sprinkled with unfussy bohemian fabrics and a mix of metals. The homeowners err toward minimalism, but well-selected zinc, aged brass, and oil-rubbed brass all live comfortably together. It was important to the couple, too, that wood tones were incorporated, and the blend—like the gray and natural oak of the kitchen stools to the dark wood of the dining chairs—plays well alongside sleek reflective finishes like the white backsplash, chunky Glassos countertop, and an oval Saarinen dining table.

According to Melissa, the biggest design challenge was striking the important balance between contemporary and cottage charm. "If one overtook the other, the overall design would simply not be successful," Melissa said. But a victory it was. "The design is restrained and somewhat minimal given the scale of the rooms, but it does feel rich and layered."

The homeowners have an incredible collection of modern art. Along with the designer, they carefully selected new frames for each of the pieces, which, once installed, brought both color and a contemporary vibe to the home.

Settle in for cozy conversation or pull up a seat at the pedestal table. An extension of the family's style, the well-furnished covered porch can be characterized as comfortable-chic.

A storybook cottage needs nothing less than an idyllic setting, and this perennial property is just that. With climbing roses, flowering trees, and a lovely white fence, the garden adds picture-perfect charm to this Connecticut home.

Tennessee Treasure

FULLY FUNCTIONAL AND WITH NO SHORTAGE OF COMFORTS, THIS GUEST SPACE HIDDEN AWAY IN A TENNESSEE FARMHOUSE IS NOTHING LESS THAN A TRUE RETREAT.

Just north of Nashville, Tennessee, hidden among vibrant green farmland, a sprawling modern farmhouse welcomes homeowner Dr. Jeannie Beauchamp's friends and family to come and recharge away from the strain of everyday life. But with only an antique log cabin to offer lodging, Jeannie found herself looking to add more space for guests.

The solution? Converting a storage attic in the main home into a 750-square-foot guest cottage perfect for offering respite to loved ones. "Most importantly, we wanted to create a relaxing retreat that could host multiple guests, brighten up the space, and utilize the small footprint we had to work with," says interior designer Connie Vernich. "It was important that we personalize the space so Jeannie felt that it was a part of who she is."

Working within the limited square footage, architect Sharon Pigott and builder Steve Griffey created a space that included everything a visitor could need, including a kitchen and living area, as well as cozy bedroom spaces. Once they were done, Connie covered every room in neutrals and an updated farmhouse style designed to enhance relaxation. "Jeannie loves neutrals and nature-inspired items, so we did a lot of light linens, soft wools, fresh striped fabrics, and natural art," she says.

These elements soften the edges of the contemporary spirit that Connie paired with the design's farmhouse base, resulting in a space that feels balanced and refreshing. "Given that this property is farmland, we knew that farmhouse style was the right direction to go in," Connie says. "But we wanted to give the ubiquitous elements that make that style so popular a fresh look." Details like modern-style barn doors and shiplap installed on the diagonal help update the style, keeping things interesting no matter where you look.

In the living room, black, white, and taupe stripes on the throw pillows and drapes are the perfect detail to elevate the strikingly simple design founded on a calming color palette. "Jeannie wanted this space to be a true getaway from the hustle and bustle," Connie says. "The crisp but neutral palette evokes relaxation and peace."

Injecting a dash of color into the living area, Nashville artist Charlotte Terrell created a custom painting "reminiscent of the landscape of East Tennessee, where the homeowner is originally from," says Connie.

Connie also incorporated a number of Jeannie's antiques and family pieces, like the sign above the apron-front sink that came from the street where the homeowner was raised. Below, an oak sink base built to look like a restored antique is set into the wall, tying in the kitchen island designed to mimic an antique table. "As a former adjunct professor of historical architecture," Connie says, "I love mixing old and new."

The antique-style elements find balance in white custom cabinets that conceal a full refrigerator, freezer, dishwasher, coffee machine, and more. "It really is hard to believe how much is in this small space," Connie says, noting that every comfort was considered during the design.

And that dedication to comfort is undeniable in the master bedroom—Connie's favorite space in the cottage. Plush seating and a linen-upholstered bed create the warm, cozy atmosphere that was a must for the space, while contemporary furniture pieces and standout artwork give it the tailored feel Connie wanted to create. "I love to add a little bit of surprise to a room and mix things up a bit," she says.

While there wasn't an excess of space to work with in the bunk room, the designers included a window seat not only for an added cozy corner but also as a functional spot for storage or putting on shoes. Linen drapes and jute tiebacks frame a window that looks out on the cow pastures, the perfect view for guests. "As functional as this space is," Connie says, "it is a bonus that it looks stylish, too."

While the entire guest cottage was crafted to encourage rest and rejuvenation, Connie says it was the screened-in porch that was designed for "total relaxation." From the twin-size Gloster chaise longues outfitted with performance fabrics to the fireplace made of Tennessee limestone and the natural cedar throughout the space, every element was chosen to foster a truly calming experience. "This is a place you come to read a book or have a glass of wine almost year-round," Connie says.

Despite its small size, the guest cottage is packed with functional features, fresh style, and plenty of inviting corners for enjoying time away from the daily grind—all without overwhelming the design. With the clever utilization of a subdued color palette and a careful balance of old and new elements, this unassuming attic became a hidden gem tucked away above a Tennessee farmhouse, complete with all the comforts of a good home away from home.

"The master bedroom is a perfect example of the homeowner's personality," Connie says. A modern console table tucked into a niche sits below a black-and-white photo of Steve McQueen, a favorite actor of the homeowner's. Framed pheasant feathers further reflect her personality, and extra robes, slippers, and blankets await guests within the closet.

Transported from a farm across the road and rebuilt on the homeowner's property, the one-room log cabin serves as additional lodging for out-of-town guests. Connie notes that the cabin's chimney bears the date 1804.

RESOURCES

Editor: Cindy Smith Cooper
Art Director: Jodi Rankin Daniels
Senior Copy Editor: Rhonda Lee Lother

Cover: Photography by Alexandra Haynes; styling by Maggie Griffin.

Introduction, 8–9: Text by Cindy Smith Cooper

A House of Happy Chance, 10–23: Photography by Eric Piasecki/ OTTO; text by Bethany Adams; architect: Robert O. Eggleston, 315-685-8144; builder: David Lee & Company, 315-685-8419; interior design by Thom Filicia, Thom Filicia Inc., thomfilicia.com, 212-736-6454.

Cottage on the Lake, 24–37: Photography by Donna Griffith; text by Cindy Smith Cooper; architect: Todd Reed, Reed Brothers Design & Build, 770-318-8395, reedbros.houzz.com; interior design by Amy Kent & Ryan Martin, Croma Design Inc., 416-366-9003, cromadesign.com.

A Serene Sanctuary, 38–47: Photography by Alexandra Haynes; text by Bethany Adams; interior design by Maggie Griffin, maggiegriffindesign.com.

Into the Wilds, 48–63: Photography by Heidi Long; text by Cindy Smith Cooper; builder: Malmquist Construction, 406-862-7846, malmquist.com; project manager: Andrew Barinowski.

Neutral, Naturally, 64–77: Photography by Kristen Mayfield; text by Cindy Smith Cooper; interior design by Kara Blalock, ReFresh Home, 615-472-1336, refresh-home.com; builder: Tennessee Valley Homes, 615-794-7415, tennesseevalleyhomes.com.

Worth the Wait, 78–91: Photography by David Welch; text by Bethany Adams; architect: Chuck Sullivan, sullivan + associates architects, 508-693-0500, sullivanassociatesarchitects.com; builder: Thomas Van Hollebeke and Jared Kent, Kent & Van Hollebeke Construction, Inc., 508-759-0354, kvhconstruction.com; interior design by Keren and Thomas Richter, White Arrow, thewhitearrow.com; landscape design by Barbara Lampson, 508-963-5543.

Built to Last, 92–103: Photography by Andrew Giammarco; text by Hannah Jones; architects: Steve Hoedemaker and Todd Beyerlein, Hoedemaker Pfeiffer, LLC, 206-545-8434, hoedemakerpfeiffer.com; interior design by Paula Alvarez, PB Designs.

Peace Like a River, 104–119: Photography by Paige Rumore Messina; text by Lauren Eberle; architect: Champ Webb,

C.W. Design, 615-456-2864, cwdesign.us; builder: Grove Park Construction, 615-678-7963, groveparkconstruction.com; interior design by Connie Vernich, Vernich Interiors, 615-730-6846. vernichinteriors.com.

Hidden Gem, 120–129: Photography by Dan Cutrona; text by Bethany Adams; architect: Chuck Sullivan, sullivan + associates architects, 508-693-0500, sullivanassociatesarchitects.com; builder: Harold Chapdelaine, 508-696-9966; interior design by Mary Rentschler, Rentschler & Company Interiors, 508-693-2058, rentschlerinteriors.com.

Gathering Place, 130–141: Photography by Andrew Giammarco; text by Hannah Jones; architect: Steve Hoedemaker of Hoedemaker Pfeiffer, LLC, 206-545-8434, hoedemakerpfeiffer. com; interior design by Tim Pfeiffer of Hoedemaker Pfeiffer, LLC.

Life on Cedar Hill, 142–155: Photography by Paige Rumore Messina; text by Cindy Smith Cooper; interior design by Julie Couch, Julie Couch Interiors, 615-873-1832, juliecouch.com; kitchen design by Sarah Avery, Town and Country Kitchens, 615-337-5865.

Building Together, 156–169: Photography by Jim Bathie; text by Bethany Adams; builder: Tim Gulledge, Trizone Homes, 205-218-0533, trizonehomes.com.

Home for the Family, 170–183: Photography by Mac Jamieson; text by Hannah Jones; renovations: Joseph Smaha, Smaha Building, LLC, 205-966-9011, smahabuilding.com; interior design by Shea Bryars, Shea Bryars Design, 205-533-2268, sheabryarsdesign.com.

Modern Luxury, 184–195: Photography by Kelli Boyd; text by Lauren Eberle; interior design by Kelley McRorie, KS McRorie Interior Design, 843-757-2529, ksmcrorieinteriordesign.com.

A New Story to Tell, 196–207: Photography by Jane Beiles; text by Lauren Eberle; architect: Louise Brooks, Brooks & Falotico, brooksandfalotico.com; builder: Rich Rosano, RRBuilders, rrbuilders.com; interior design by Melissa Lindsay, Pimlico Interiors, 203-972-8166, pimlicointeriors.com.

Tennessee Treasure, 208–217: Photography by Paige Rumore Messina; text by Bethany Adams; architect: Sharon Pigott, Sharon Pigott Architect, 615-400-0522, sharonpigottarchitect.com; builder: Steve Griffey, Steve Griffey Construction, 931-368-1326; interior design by Connie Vernich, Vernich Interiors, 615-730-6846, vernichinteriors.com.